The Face of the Earth

AF624776

Hareer A Al-Qaragolie

BookLeaf Publishing

Presentation by *BookLeaf Publishing*

Web: www.bookleafpub.com

E-mail: info@bookleafpub.com

ISBN: 9789357441841

First edition 2023

To mama, baba, Tala, and Hamza

You bring me home

PREFACE

"my people my people
I thought
the fall would
kill me
but it only
made me real."
— Ocean Vuong, Time Is a Mother

A Whisper

sugar coated rose petals
a pinch of salt
swirling for a taste

the strength of silk
tugs your tongue
left and right
hugging your lips
in awe

the skeleton of my name
holds bonds
you try to pull
limb from limb
as you pronounce it

taste my name
melting in your tongue
with tea and mint
Burning your teeth
soaked in cardamom

my name is the sound of an exhale,
a whisper,
that tickles your cheeks

to vibrate your tongue
in forgotten places,
feel them dance

our letters protect me
from a heavy heart.
they embrace me
when you see me as unspoken

Secrets etched within the
soft exterior of each letter.
Secretes my ancestors whisper.
They rest in the space between
each ر you cant roll

I abandon my first letter
adjust the rolls of my tongue
to make my name
a perfect fit
for your mouth

Silk,
A gift so unloved
it falls in wrong hands
of merchants and travelers
on Her route

Silk,
drapes their fingertips

of gold platted arms
hiding in firm shells

Silk,
hard to swallow
the gulp of her magnitude.
You cant have my name.

ر – The letter R in Arabic is pronounces with a roll

Build

Cherries replacing olive pips
and syrup
as she spits incantations soaked with summer
dews
and windy breath

stacks of newspapers and coupons on a basket
we think came with the house,
old golden embroidered plates with silver linings
on the outer borders.

the smell of pomegranate molasses,
cayenne, cardamom,
mistika, wood, sage,
lathered with honey, mint, and leather.

the wind shrieks through the openings of the
windows
making their way through the forbidden
wooden cabinet of flutes,
martini and shot glasses
in a house that doesn't drink

nicotine, burnt coal, and apricots with her
homemade sourdough

That burned her hijab
and sugary plum jam
tucked in imperishable and unreachable jars

lanterns as tall as i with chrystofil crystals, gold,
and rusty iron
to fill the mystic room of crimson red
and blood orange ceiling with glue stains
from tapestries of bismillah

graphite tables and white squared kitchen floors
with stains of curry that bring us home

diplomas that smell of lost years
stacks of negatives and scratched cassettes
with broken hairbrushes
and chipped istikans.
this house intimidates time as He defies our
suffering
yet bring us ease.

snowy white dews creeping in the window.
so different from fluttering eyes to the sight
of the light creeping in
With the intend to blind

i don’t see the hilal up here,
nor get kisses that feel Arabic.

To build a house is to bring your land to you.

drops of wax, baby breaths and a scent of
mama’s bukhar
blessing my ears with
Slow inhales

Its not enough to burn olive oil and
make white coffee.
Bliss is licking sugar off of our fingertips
scraping the edge of a floral table cloth
that aged better

I ask, where do I belong,
He says, in between the spaces of
each word in the quran.
In the pauses between each kneel,
And after each sigh of the shahadeh.

To build a house is to bring your land to you.

O's

Saha
Health
Ala albik
On your heart

How do I explain to a stranger
I pray for their hearts
in sickness or in health

My language carries collective pain
The cries of an Olive tree
Older than the Occupation

My language is poetry
that loves the writer more,
carrying the red and black threads
Interweaving our dresses
and the new romantics
of our Old letters
falling for the lust of its strokes

Saha
Health
Ala albik
On your heart

How do I explain my language was displaced
Like us
And that I treat you
better than they treated
Arabic, that makes our tongue
Wanting more of its aftertaste
Craving for every word that caresses
Our taste buds
Penetrating our ears with
I love you

Ana wala inta
Me and never you

How do I explain to a stranger
that I dream of the day
of taking their pain
to never have them feel it

My language lives in loops
Like the O's of my hair and history of cutting it
Like the scorching sun that shone on their graves
Like the rings that make our baskets on our
heads
Like the hoops of our endurance

Ya rooh alby
The soul of my heart

Inta eeyunee
You are my eyes

My eyesight is yours
to see the colors I surround you with.
The dark is afraid of my language
It feels threatened by the way
it makes you feel color
As the wind carries its words
with ease.
The earth sighs in relief, Hamdillah

Arabic taught me that I love you.
with every inch of my body
moving in harmony
working with every bone
to spread my blood to my lungs,
counting every breathe

for you

Sabah il kheir
Good morning
Tisbah Alah Kheir,
Good night

How do I explain I wish for a stranger
To have a morning of peace
And to sleep in ever lasting grace

I love you
Comes around in o’s.

Ellipses

The bitterness that resides
In my ink does not
belong in my
Tongue.
The foreign aftertaste
ages like wine,
Reminding me of it's bittersweet
intent to be familiar.

The pain of the sting
is a promise of life,
as the pen caresses
foreign letters and
familiar blood
alike
to circulate the distance and geographies
of freedom

Let the Oud stain my neck
Oud stain my neck
Henna mask my hair
Rose water linger in my breath
as I inhale the rhythms of our letters

screaming from neglect

My Borrowed Tongue Wont Erase
the cardamom from our tea,
the smoke from our bukhar,
the whispering chills of Tilaweh
the strokes that dress our letters
and the ellipses of our resilience

Cut my tongue,
It bleeds Baghdad.
It hides in
The liberty that I never knew

Bukhar – incense

The Sleeping Elephant

I'm roaming around the 'orangery room'
In a pink haze of chandelier lights and glaring
eyes
Of 'I'll be there for you' s
In the therapy school room,
Hopes of carrying the weight of others
To cancel what we carry ourselves

Figures of clay hands and paint splattered faces
Circle around the Iranian stained carpet
To 'feel and not think' as we pick
Figures from unconscious minds for our sand
tray,
What is a heart if not a darling to kill?

In the middle of the unconventional porcelain
miniatures
And action figures of stories our kids will
Forever live through, I see you.
What is a heart if not a darling to kill?

A baby elephant of petal ears and fingernail long
Trunk rests in my hand as it will rest in my
project,
Buried as its eyes close in grief.

The lines on its futures stretch along
It faded discolored body that show
Tentative years in death,
Stories of wisdom not shared,
Hours of sun in the womb,
Ingrown ivory before piano keys.
Brushed eyebrows with no hair
Pink lips with no kiss,
Blushed ears that say it was alive.

My shaky palms carry the elephant in a choked hiccup
As I walk to its wake to my sand tray,
remembering you.
Placing him on the edge of a cliff,
next to the plastic swan swimming
In the sand stream
next to the yellow feather the
Kids will call Nigel and Bambi toy
glaring at the sight of the reaper

But the elephant was resting
on the wooden man made earth,
on the Edge of the stream,
In melancholy and awe as the ducks swim
To an ending.
To turn death into rest is
how I live through you.
With love, pink ears and ink drawn closed eyes

That marry the ground as the gazelle holds back
The tiger with an elastic band
During the funeral that never happened.

The Face of the Earth

the face of the earth

fell on his lap like

a pool of petals dripped in sweet sweet blood

hiding in nectraine.

his face crafted by years of the battle field

of knife licking strawberry shaving cream

and moldy bread to break the fast

that forced his hands to grow thorns,

tongue to call mercy, and pupils to turn black

He calls her the face of the earth, a song

he lost among his dreams found within

a heartstopping youth of levantine streets,

and creamy carols of melted turkish delights,

swinging among Baghdad's clock in shrieks of evil

the face of the earth wales as he holds her,

waves of pain crashing eloquently on her skin

through his touch, they heave as as they feel

what others dont.

As time drapes his cloak of unforseeable hues of color,

to paint every visit as a new guest we dont recognize.

we offer him all we have, put our heads and neck

on a platter as he sighs in smoky breaths of horror

reminding us of our numbered moments, taking us back when

my small figure held the weight of his pain gladly.

My father planted the earth on my face

but hes the moon, the sun, and all its stars that
bring me to life,

to art, to aimless dreams that do not know of
hollow shells

and peaky eyes and fleeting jabs of peril, in
exchange for his veins.

I'll give up the earth to stop him bleed, plant my
face

in the wall, and cement my feet for him to smell
the gardenia again,

and break the barbwires that pinch his skin to
grow wysteria on his back.

Leeluwat

She mends the past
That soaked my blue blanket
With bloody foreheads
and cumin
Her voice is a river,
a current
blowing the smoke
that hid Baghdad

her lullabies break shells
of hurt,
of songless dreams
and post war money

I wish to taste
From her eyes
Tears of liquid luck
Falling from
Blue laces and
Golden edges
peeling from
Ballroom halls,
Crystal skies,
Pinks silk sheets,
Lusty pomegranates,

Dates falling from grace
for years,
from trees of
heavenly heights

Salt the wounds
as time pours it.
Cover the bullet holes
Of empty years
with cold jokes
etched on stone staircases
with tally marks

I am lost in translation at a home that was mine

Her arms twirling the spoon
in circles for zardeh
for our teeth to dance
prayers to answer
and soft hearts
to carry the weight

But all I taste
Is the bitter black ice
masking as nutmeg
for a better life
in colors

but color does not taste

of pickled mangoes
olive trees, purple dews
red sand and the touch of motherhood
and death

Leeluwat leeluwat

My slumber rests in baghdad
my eyes in amman
i can't have both

zardeh – Iraqi dessert

Honest

The chipped purple cups, torn embroidered curtains, off white cabinets, silver plated frames and broken toaster smelt of stories I'll never hear again. Tales that carried the weight on your shoulders as they pushed your spine towards me.

Stories that slowed your steps and made your eyelids so heavy, but smile so effortless with the thought of each memory.

I embraced your skeleton figure, wishing the bones would interlace with mine to drag me seven feet under as Azrael blows the horn and engulfed you in a kiss.

It's Friday morning. The steam blinded your glasses as the kettle screamed. You knew I liked my beans pealed. You'd sneak a bite after we finished eating even though you said you were full every time. You would adjust your kufi, slide it to the right, take seven steps to the stove and turn to look at me. your eyes were knives as a ray if light hits them to remind me of your divinity. I wish they would still cut through me to shake and shiver as hard as I did when you asked for the fork.

I fell further with each bite as you sat in front me. The sound of steam and cutlery echoed through the air to signal how far away you were from me. Sitting in front of you was to swallow your magnitude that eloquently grasped my neck in a tight squeeze. Our chewing was louder than our stares and colored in our differences. The space between our years gifted us silence that never hurt, but spoke volumes from knowing I will never understand the scale of loss, pain, and glory that engulfed your figure. Our gap reminds me of my naïve hands and innocent eyes that tell of nothing.

You blew six kisses on your hand in my direction. They went right through your mask as I took several steps backwards to catch my breath. Ill waste all my breaths for you to swallow to give you what our biggest enemy of all, time, didn't.

You raised a hand from your pockets of a robe I dream of you still.

when you dream of the dead, it affirms that they are living. I didn't allow you to come into mine.

I protected myself from the pinching reality of ever feeling your emptiness. I could flip quranic pages everyday for you and never do your prayers justice. Allah doesn't eat up my voice. He swallows your prayers like zamzam, a taste so lustful. He doesn't quench for my empty words and hollow sobs of pity.

He lost your readings. They were so heavy it closed your eyes and dug my head to the ground from the weight of your palms. With each stressed word, each pronounced syllable and stroke, you elevated me with you.

I inhaled the life back into me when I felt your ghost that night. I screamed "Im not ready Im not ready" and sighed with a release that freed me. Noor woke up heaving when she saw you drenched in pink water. Mama saw you in the passenger seat when she was 23 again; telling her you liked zaatar on your chicken. Baba saw your piety through your six daughters as he lives everyday to raise his. You saw us raw. I couldn't allow you to see me so naked. To dream of you is not to resurrect your presence, its to affirm the deadening of you and I.

I saw you in a garden that wasn't mine, but was so familiar. Endless vines of grape leaves and apple trees towered our heads to make us feel small. The smell of leek and gardenia put me in a ray of panic. The narrow walk composed of three cement tiles and a 6 inch green fence to protect the paper wind blowers as they danced. It was Baghdad. That rusty swing overlooked the date trees behind me, you pointed to our haress to climb on a summer mornings of 60 degrees.

I saw you twice. When I approached, you held your arms that complimented your toothless smile and oversized glasses that hung from the blue debrie of your robe. I yelled finally, what did I just say? You smiled for the last time. You left me the same way you came in my dream, with ease. I screamed finally, again? I ran to you as much as I could. Dreams hinder our true needs. I fought my paralyzed figure that failed to embrace you; the space I felt in your kitchen was the space that I craved to occupy again.

As I approached you I saw you for the second time. You were on a chair with a suit on. Same suit in from auntie Dalia's photo albums. I held your face, finally, and caressed your thick eyebrows in all your beauty. Can eyes lock in a dream? Your wrinkles stretched to disappear from my touch.

I felt your fingers get stuck in my hair again from the wet curls, you yelled at me cause it was cold. Dreams don't tell the weather, but the rain pierced my skin as I felt each drop bite my arms. The gut wrenching guilt and heavy sigh rest on my throat still. I woke up gutted as the wires from the light bulb sticking from my ceiling in Abu Fadi's apartment stretched to interlace with my body through my mouth, pulling me closer as my neck fell backwards.

Can I call a dream mine if I died in it?

The wires sucked the finger linking dreams that were soaked in the grease of fish oil and sunny side ups on yellow rice with raisins served on a tin plate to eat another soul and beat a mother's heart

Rain smudged the letters of incoherent sounds and erasing the maps and traces of coming home. I saw you twice.

Madeeha

She watered the black iris
Growing on the intersection.
With her last drop to keep her awake
From the sleepless night, she drove
With one hand on the steering wheel
And the other to pin her hijab.
She promised to drink today.

She watered the black iris
emerging between her tires in the garage.
The heat held its weight on her shoulders
As she carried the drops of the water from
The clay pot she leaves on the baranda for the rain
as a gift to soak the infinite drought of the middle east.
She promised to drink today.

She watered the black iris
In the middle of the night
To keep her dreams purple
She could've sworn they used to be red
for they stained her jedo's palm trees
In memory of a land they claimed was not hers.
She promised to drink today.

She watered the black iris
Growing in the playground with sugar.
she washed the cuts of the boy's head
with what's left of her water and
added sugar to her old tea for the iris
as she hid her burned knuckles from
making samoon for the bus drivers.

She replenished the earth with her sadaqa
And complemented her with silence
madeeha

She watered the black iris
To have them pluck it.
the price of sadaqa
is to never feel like it is.

Baranda – balcony
Jedo – grandfather
Samoon – Iraqi flatbread
Sadaqa – one of the pillars of Islam, to give without seeking a substitute in return

Blind Safety

Pardon my hello,
I didn't know you
were prone to peace
Assalamu Aleikom

Excuse my gratitude
as you roll your eyes
Hamdilla

Apologies for my care
you hate when I wish you well
Inshallah

Forgive my eyes,
they are not blue,
for that I am blind to you

I beg you to
Ignore my lips,
I cannot
disregard the "T"

You find safety in
my pale skin,
for the Middle Eastern

sun refuses
to kiss it,

You feel ease
from my hair,
for I don't cover it
like you think
I should

You glorify
my blue veins,
for they hide
the redness of ,
my Arab blood

You stare at
my freedom,
because it gives
you purpose
to teach me
your own

But please,
be aware,
my teachings
do not preach
ignorance,
because when
you didn't

Bombs came
instead of rain
Bullets carved my walls
instead of
my drawings
we breathed
gunpowder
From teta's cooking
Instead of seasoning

I choose to
stay patient
with you
for mama
taught me

I choose to
take care
of you
because my
teachings
guided Me

I choose to
stand by you,
because my
Quran told me

I choose to
forgive you,
for my pillars
sought me

I choose
to accept your
hate, because
I've been taught
to love you

So please tell me,
how much hate can you give
to teach me how to love

Leightweight

Heavy Jasmine
Falling on white cotton bedsheets
Piercing through the light
Each petal is a burden
Unmeasurable weight that breaks stems
As it breaks your spine
Weight from the relentless rain causing
thunderbolts
To clasp between pillows
The impact shattered the glass on my stomach
Wishing it hit my ribs instead.
As you left I picked the pieces, missing little
specs that cut deeper
Than your words that got lost in between the
floorboards,
Forever hiding from the truth
You heave relentlessly trying to work the puzzle

As folds form on our skin and plaster
covers the holes on the wall,
you'd stumble on the glass along with the petals
Soft, lightweight, and tired.
Words you've never been told.
You have a choice to wash the blood stain

and unmask your hate with the biggest gift I
gave.
To keep and be kept

Playing House

she fumbles with her palms while i fidget

wondering if i should text him, or should she

because im the daughter and the devil rests

on my tongue to run whenever he wants

but i can't

3eib Habibty, girls don't do that

As father's bruises piled up for the vultures to pick

daughters to peel and wife to suck the gory details

you can go upstairs whenever you want and lie about praying

while the kettle screeches your arrival but

i cant help but think im the missing puzzle, the one who should scarafise a state of mind that melts like qamr al deen to be be thrown in a place

confusing hell with high waters

waiting for the smoke to sweep both of you

as I count sheep in my sleep

day by day and jump (tic tac toe) on the pavement

drenched in shisha coals the sun gifted us, she gives many

gifts we don't need in Baghdad

a playful war waiting to erupt from its muzzle

While we breathe the news gently and

Carry our mother's gossip on our back

And Stich our mouths closed when baba asks about our day

Mirror

What would the poets dwell on to write the scene?

Of a beating heart laid on a cobblestone pavement

as the heat poached our dried olives

This way to hone a dead craft!

Being Arab is living everyday as a martyr

To drape the constellations on your back and paint a picture as you dive into the dark loom, hands reaching out from the shadowy damp pits of despair for an ancestor you forgot to dedicate a prayer to

Our winds blow the sand dunes accumulated with tears that carry stories

Stories we hid on purpose to not outshine the eagles' eyes as they eat our hearts, wet our dreams, and water the soil with heavy blood that melt into our skin

That's when we remember

We melted ourselves with theirs

Broken Trail

im picking nettles off my arms

wondering when will it be me that you'll walk with

down the winvenhoe trail

that fill your eyes with the sublime

a beauty so fragile, so petrifying it filled

my eyes with gore i cherish. blood

our month couldnt forge.

you pick the pulp from the juice and

scratch the skin off the nettles.

removing me is removing an impurity

that my mom worked so hard to keep clean.

with high horse necks and black owl eyes

they use the name of of our maker in vain to
keep us apart.

whoever drew the line of maps forgot to trace
the red ink with love.

to love an arab is to peel skin of the edges of a
nail

you've been forced to pinch inside. Or that's
what

you will tell me once you keep your promises of

always understanding why bebe pours tea in 50
degree weather

or why baba calls me baba, or how

we hide pokemon cards under the persian carpet

to keep them from our cousins.

you promised to cook your rice with cardemom,

turn the quality street container into a sewing
kits

as a joke that turned into a generation.

to say amoot beech too show me that dying in
me

is the only way we'll see tomorrow.

I want you to open the powder satchet of tang in
ramadan

without explaining why our stomachs sigh for
sundown,

and why we wait for the lunar calender's
anoucement

that stops us from swallowing water, a rule you
religiously refuse

as i breathe to fill and prove your conviction

of what it means to be healthy in Allah's eyes.

i lost you in the ink,

in the fold,

and in the patterns that draped my existence,

decorated my eyes with a glimmer

so far from you, you saw cateracts

in all that created me.

i felt it all and then nothing evermore

the full elasticity of love kept us intertwined in lecture rooms

and broken dreams of values we never chose.

tugging on heart strings that

never weave themselves

as the laces curl up to tie our necks.

ill wait for the rain to fall off the bluebells,

and watch the fog smoke up my kitchen window

to feel time as it stays still in my home.

you didnt pick the nettles, you scratched the skin

Write Down I Am Arab

I write my name in Arabic to not make my hand forgot it was born to draw letters and their stroked from the right. To remind myself of the orientation I was assimilated to. All For a better life. The left side of the paper feels almost too familiar and it's frightening. To put the colonizers language next to your mother . They push and tug on each other in your mouth, head, hands, and heels. A struggle worth a victory. worth losing a home. A lustrous future. A vision that is already attainable in my fantastical idea of an Arab life that exists between the lines of Kanafani and Darwish. But there is no such thing. I write my name to remember, we don't exist. A waste of time yearning for a fleeting moment to reminisce a past we don't know. A past I don't know. I write my name in Arabic to remember Living is a right, and To carry yourself on your land is a stolen privilege. I learned the difference early on. And I caress the ground aimlessly every day, imagining what it's like to die in the name of Arabic. For to be buried in its soil is the closest I will get to living.

Self (blue) Pity (gold)

the strength that pulled our backs upwards

is derived from the same energy that dragged us

to put our boundaries in hellfire, watch them

in satisfying as the amber of our love scream

of confusion as loud as i did.

Angels eyes pouring out salt

And milky tears that taste of venom

fooling you all

as i bathe the blood of the victim.

You threw the glass on my ribs

while your curls

swiftly decorated his face

replacing the intent

that allah planted in me.

I wish it tore through me instead

Cause I was too busy emptying my cup

to be there for someone

who never filled me up

as I poured

I love you's

That's the only thing wrong about you

But you made it clear

The evil eye you threw at me

colores the space of our fitted borders

we ignored

with gold and blue

as you sit in the middle of the black pool,

iris pouring

its water in my throat

as you hold me in ribbons of envy

tying our necks like wired circuits

struggling to breath in

tentative years Where we danced on the clouds

But the heavy weight of our soles just threw me to the ground

covered in the blues of Beirut

Of people you forced me to loose

For loving you the way that I did with a label

of “i may destroy myself for you”

my martydom wasnt honorable

to fix up your braids,

pick up the specs from your cat's paw,

or color my white canvas

until you painted it gold

Your favourite on purpose

I protected you from what they thought of you

And never let them choke on the lies that I

Thought weren't true

Of how you treated me less than you ever did

And I made excuses

instead of listen to the cups that

clasped loudly impatiently

between your fingertips

with your green chipped nail polish

that filled your tea with flakes

of rage

i asked God if he had anything to say to me

I looked for his words in coffee grains from

Aunties cups, i hear him laugh and i join

replying with blasphemy

the price of being pure is resentment,

even the untouched scream in lust they never
knew

from the sight.

Candy hearts

Candy hearts

Of cherry

Hubba bubba

And lemon drops scattered on barb wires t

To play candy crush

Is to get lost in the glow

Angel wings they never wanted

Sucking the red and yellow from the

Wrappers takes them back to eid

At bebes

Come play pick the gun drops

From the barb wires! And decorate your

Stomach with delicious gun powder

That fills your appetite like an explosion

In the name of American exceptionalism,

We eat your candy

drink your **Milk and Soda**

favoring the rasberry chased cool aid

and grenadine

with gas that pokes our throats with bubbles

that bleed cherry syrup when it pops,

they sell the taste of a revolution

that made you wish we ate more.

Make me Live

I still hear it

Droplets of rain on the blue and yellow

Pavements bouncing off the circular pumps

Of cinder blocks, making it hard to

wake and breathe as

The small of wet dirt hits my head.

It's remind you of flooding.

You close your eyes and i can see it,

Sitting with your dad and your sisters

As you chew on your shawarma stuck

In your dark green Suzuki in traffic.

I live it through you, each stop

Each petal falling from a daisy invaded house,

Each saved button on your torn dresses

They ripped from you.

Fallen candy that hit our heads

Is a feeling I crave, a celebration you manifest,

The luluwing that escapes you throat is a release

From the ever soft tongue, they used

Sugar to numb it. Waiting to escape

The love trampled between your tonsils.

Close your eyes, take a breath blow on each lid
and kiss me, bring me Baghdad

Prick my index finger with burnt needle you put
on

That candle the night of Zakaria.

Make a wish Mama, kneel in the rain and say
Allahabad akbar, look up.

You ask Him yo enter you for me, as I chew gum

And flip glossy pages while fighting

With my J zipper.

Burn incense and twirl 3 times in front

Of the stove.

Enter new places with your right feet,

hold your sister's hands as you jump

one foot up.Then the other.

Make me live.

The rain never stopped its rhythm,

Nor was it shy from flooding our neighborhood

As you handed the cars your plate.

Give mama, give all you have to bring your home to me.

Knowing it will never come to you.

How do I tell you of the humility of sujood?

You know my tongue

But have you felt the humility of sujood?

Your eyes tell of of sights I've seen young

Of a land lost that felt forced to rejoice.

You can't find God in the trenches like my dad as he foraged

In the pits of a begger's peach, in the bites of easy peel oranges, or in

The wallet sized picture of Jedo's shriveled smile

I kneel, strike my heart as I lean

My head on the floor and shiver from the deja vu

Of nothing

Of how big

How Light

It is to surrender your name

That felt like a gulp

Resting on my back

When it was just a spec.

So isjud, my love

Let out a wale of vulnerability

Of your existence in a vaccuum filled with temporalities

If not to keep me to remind you

We are souls floating by

Angels don’t exist

the ray shot Through

The curtain to remind

Us of the danger

Of the grave. So what

If you break my bones

And gnaw them to stick candle wax

On my shoulder blades,

Build wings to throw me for the next

Person and melt to my demise.

What if I fly to heaven

Briefly and never again?

The taste doesn’t rest on my eyelids

The same way my tongue doesn’t see

the fire in your breath,

Or hear the heartbreak

Of your knuckles that

Trickles my love between the spaces,

Too scared to flutter our arms or else its the end

In our faces, a death we wrote to fill gaps

In our teeth. I wanted to paint Lillies and

White roses on the mirror to show you its lying
to you.

But maybe the paint was too bright,

The canvas too big, it lied to me

And you warned me as you broke wood

For my back before the last push.

I just wanted to see myself there.

Mama blows on my face to wake up and

I can tell you'll take a step back if I do.

So dream, forge, and leave knowing you killed
the doe

While you choked on her blood and carved my
name

In your neck, forever, poison in nectar.

I’ll be There

Our ghosts left residues in every corner

Of this flat, wales of my knowing telling

Our ending before we run off.

I often wish I was a fool

In the present. But the future tense

is harder in my mouth, Why?

The hardest pill to swallow rests

on the specs on your shirt,

Falling on my palms, engulfing me

with what I already know

Is in front of me.

The universe is a restless mother

dictating her natural disasters

on her most beloved.

You talked to her on the phone

on a night of hazy blues

From the emerging lights

humbling us into living

In moments that tether our expectations.

Mother cares about order

more than our ease,

Weaving her destruction in tearful adoration.

I didn't reach her threshold

because I kneel to Allah,

I fast from sunrise to sundown

And exhale hamdillah.

Mother cares about order.

So hold on love, will you?

I allow you to cling to the ropes

you so begged me to cut

with beautiful locks that strengthen

The maps of Syria.

The ghosts don't whisper

or hiccup in the walls,

Nor do they turn off the fun,

They just hear me shiver,

Teeth clattering As the vibrations

leave us unfinished.

Our years curate a memory

Of a dream by design.

And I see a glimps of my commissioned piece

In your eyes, that I had to sell.

So keep giving pieces of your heart,

hold the paper thin dreams

that rests in poetry.

Embrace the heat of it all.

Don’t resent mother as I

head the other way.

Because in the streams of the chess valley,

The ripples of frozen rain

On the windows, the frosts on your eyelids,

The in between and ingenious banter

Of i love you more and catching the one

Who got away

When the time is right
I’ll find you in between the winds of our lands
We’ll be walking in fields of peonies growing
around clovers

Dropping their petals to quench our feet
For a path long overdue.
across the lines there's painting

from a splintered brush that sheds pieces of a
home
I'll be there.

www.ingramcontent.com/pod-product-compliance
Lightning Source LLC
Chambersburg PA
CBHW051735130826
49812CB00033B/872
9789357441841